# SCHIRMER'S LIBRARY
## OF MUSICAL CLASSICS

Vol. 2109

T0066590

# PIANO MASTERWORKS

# EARLY INTERMEDIATE LEVEL

## 144 Pieces by 22 Composers

ISBN 978-1-4950-0688-3

# G. SCHIRMER, Inc.

DISTRIBUTED BY

HAL•LEONARD®
CORPORATION

7777 W. BLUEMOUND RD. P.O. BOX 13819 MILWAUKEE, WI 53213

www.musicsalesclassical.com
www.halleonard.com

# CONTENTS

## MUZIO CLEMENTI

## JEAN-BAPTISTE DUVERNOY

## ALBERT ELLMENREICH

## EDVARD GRIEG

## CORNELIUS GURLITT

## GEORGE FRIDERIC HANDEL

## STEPHEN HELLER

## LOUIS KÖHLER

(Continued on next page)

* The composer did not write a piece for letter "J."

## ROBERT SCHUMANN

## LOUIS STREABBOG

## PYOTR IL'YICH TCHAIKOVSKY

# Minuet
in G Major

Anonymous
BWV Appendix 116

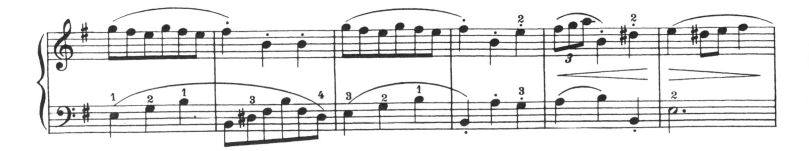

# Polonaise
## in G minor

Anonymous
BWV Appendix 119

# Musette
## in D Major

Anonymous
BWV Appendix 126

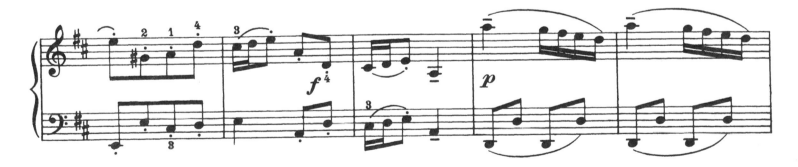

# Minuet
in D minor

Anonymous
BWV Appendix 132

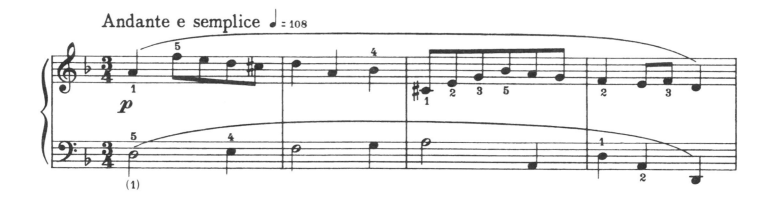

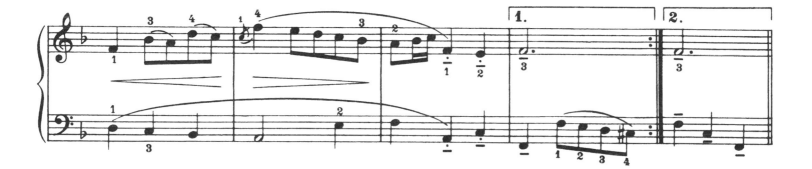

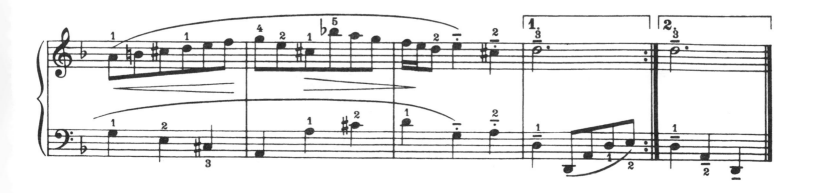

# March
## in D Major

Carl Philipp Emanuel Bach
BWV Appendix 122

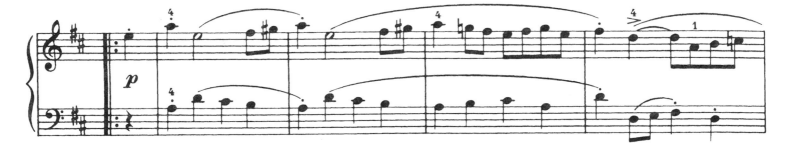

# Prelude
## in C Major

Johann Sebastian Bach
BWV 939

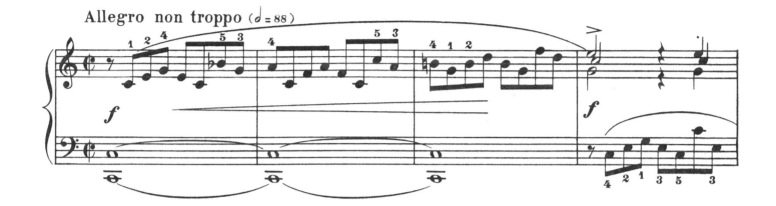

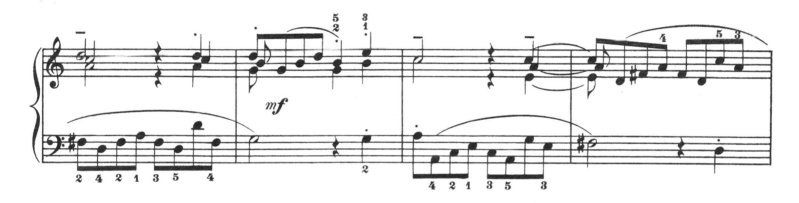

# Peasant Song
from *Ten Easy Pieces*

Belá Bartók

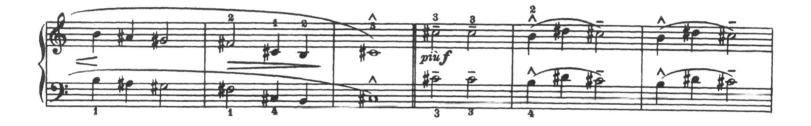

# Painful Scuffle

from *Ten Easy Pieces*

Belá Bartók

# Slovak Youth Dance

from *Ten Easy Pieces*

Belá Bartók

# Sostenuto
from *Ten Easy Pieces*

Belá Bartók

# Evening in Transylvania
from *Ten Easy Pieces*

Belá Bartók

**Tempo I**

**Vivo non rubato**

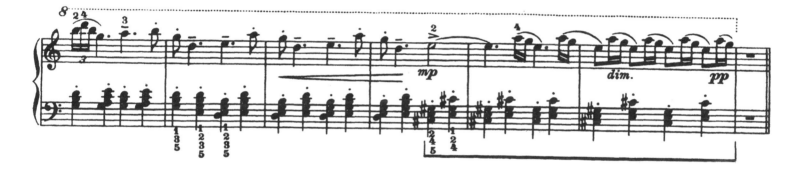

**Tempo I**

# Hungarian Folksong
## (Snow in the Town Square)
from *Ten Easy Pieces*

Belá Bartók

# Dawn
from *Ten Easy Pieces*

Belá Bartók

(1'30")

# Folksong
## (Please Say Yes)

from *Ten Easy Pieces*

Belá Bartók

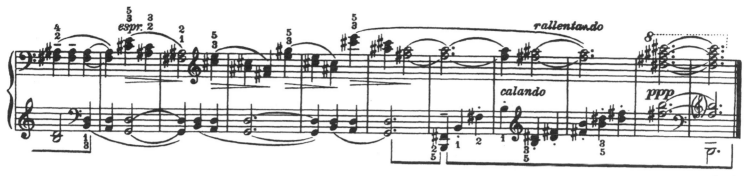

# Finger Study
from *Ten Easy Pieces*

Belá Bartók

# Sonatina
## in G Major

Ludwig van Beethoven
Anh. 5, No. 1

**Moderato**

## ROMANZE

# Écossaise
in E-flat Major

Ludwig van Beethoven
WoO 86

# Waltz
in D Major

Ludwig van Beethoven
WoO 85

# La candeur

(Frankness)

from *25 Easy and Progressive Studies*

Johann Friedrich Burgmüller
Op. 100, No. 1

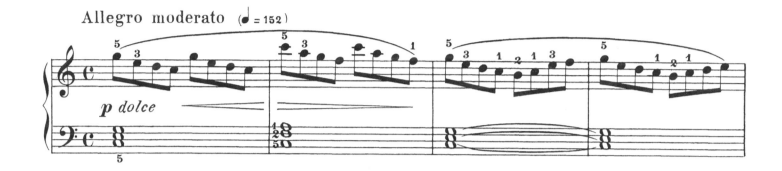

# L'arabesque

from *25 Easy and Progressive Studies*

Johann Friedrich Burgmüller
Op. 100, No. 2

Allegro scherzando ( ♩ = 152 )

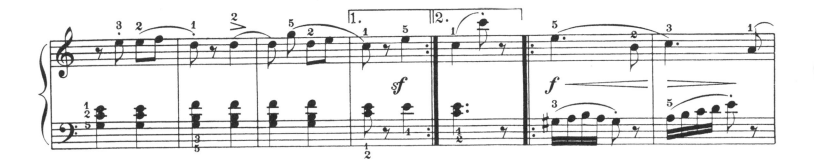

# La pastorale

from *25 Easy and Progressive Studies*

Johann Friedrich Burgmüller
Op. 100, No. 3

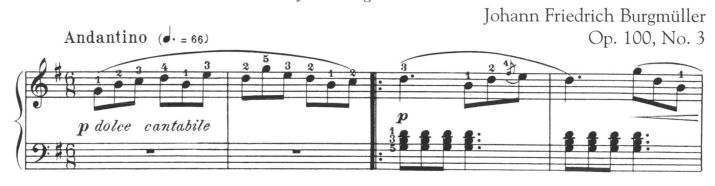

# La petite réunion

(The Little Reunion)

from *25 Easy and Progressive Studies*

Johann Friedrich Burgmüller
Op. 100, No. 4

Allegro, ma non troppo

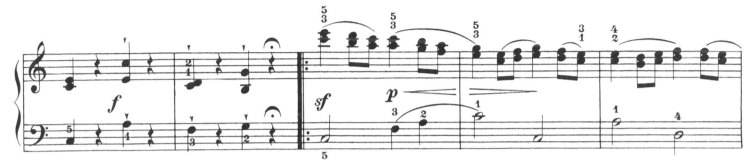

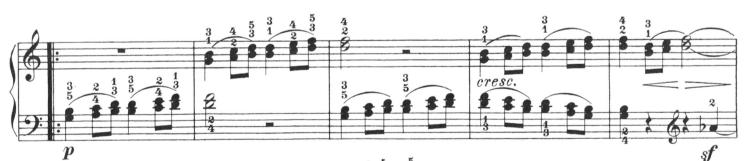

# Innocence

from *25 Easy and Progressive Studies*

Johann Friedrich Burgmüller
Op. 100, No. 5

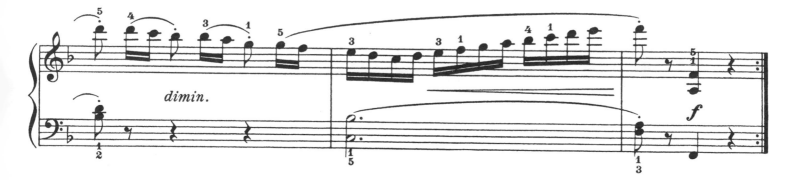

# Progrès

(Progress)

from *25 Easy and Progressive Studies*

Johann Friedrich Burgmüller
Op. 100, No. 6

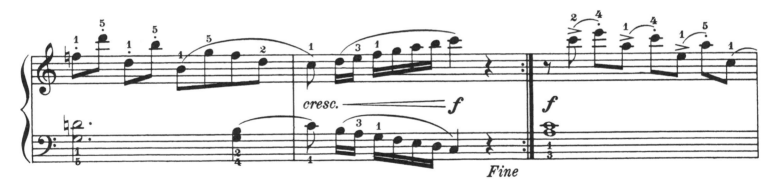

D. C.

# Le courant limpide

(The Limpid Stream)

from *25 Easy and Progressive Studies*

Johann Friedrich Burgmüller
Op. 100, No. 7

*D. C.*

# La gracieuse

(Grace)

from *25 Easy and Progressive Studies*

Johann Friedrich Burgmüller
Op. 100, No. 8

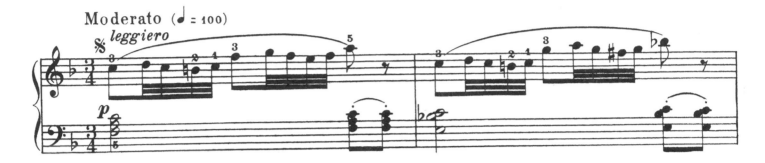

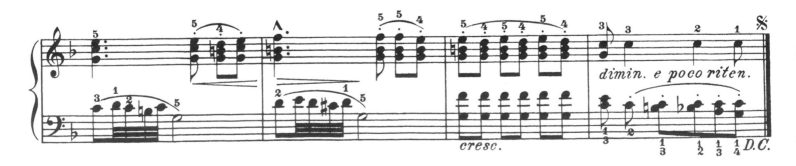

# La styrienne

from *25 Easy and Progressive Studies*

Johann Friedrich Burgmüller
Op. 100, No. 14

Mouvement di Valse (♩=176)

# Ballade

from *25 Easy and Progressive Studies*

Johann Friedrich Burgmüller
Op. 100, No. 15

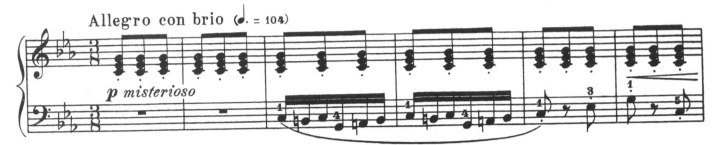

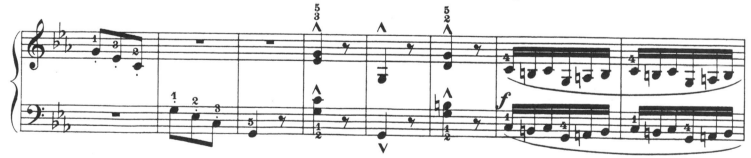

# Inquiétude
(Concern)

from *25 Easy and Progressive Studies*

Johann Friedrich Burgmüller
Op. 100, No. 18

Allegro agitato (♩ = 138)

# Ave Maria

from *25 Easy and Progressive Studies*

Johann Friedrich Burgmüller
Op. 100, No. 19

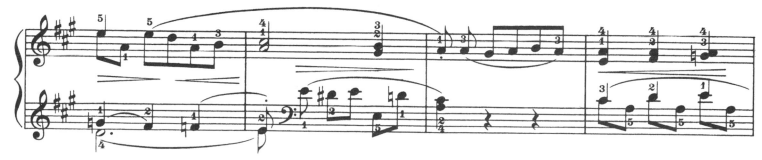

# L'harmonie des anges

(Harmony of the Angels)

from *25 Easy and Progressive Studies*

Johann Friedrich Burgmüller
Op. 100, No. 21

# Sonatina
## in C Major

Muzio Clementi
Op. 36, No. 1

Spiritoso

**Andante**

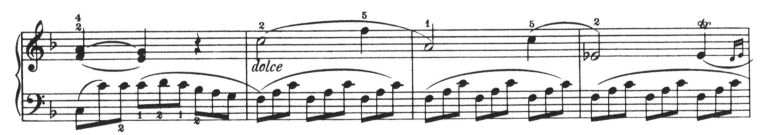

**Vivace**

# Study in A Major
### in A Major
from *25 Elementary Studies*

Jean-Baptiste Duvernoy
Op. 176, No. 15

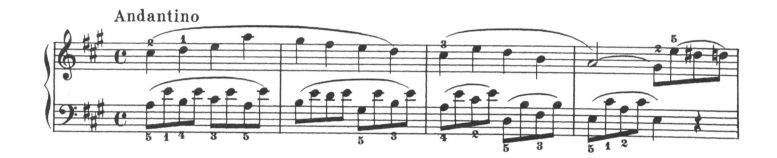

# Spinning Song

Albert Ellmenreich
Op. 14, No 4

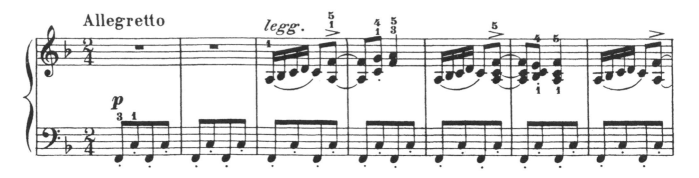

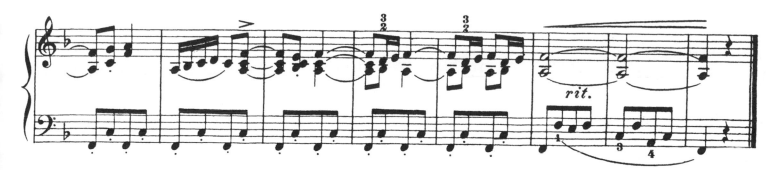

# Watchman's Song
## from *Lyric Pieces*

Edvard Grieg
Op. 12, No. 3

**Molto Andante e semplice**

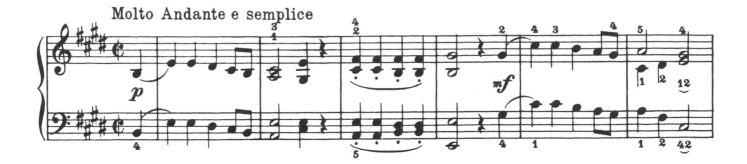

**Intermezzo**

# National Song

from *Lyric Pieces*

Edvard Grieg
Op. 12, No. 8

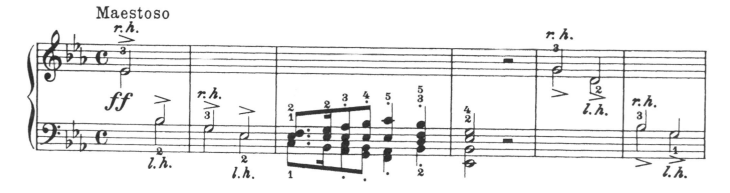

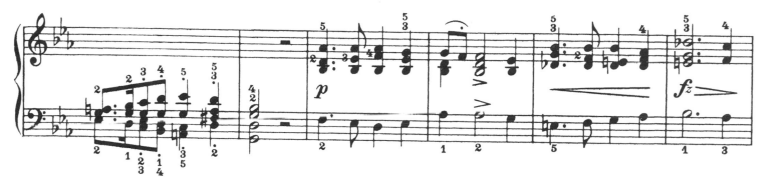

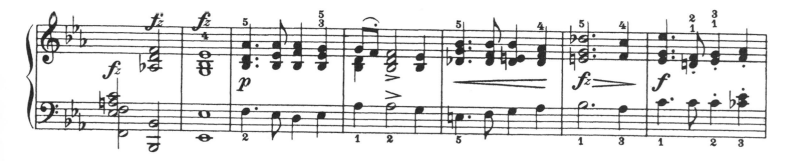

# Sailor's Song

from *Lyric Pieces*

Edvard Grieg
Op. 68, No. 1

**Allegro vivace e marcato**

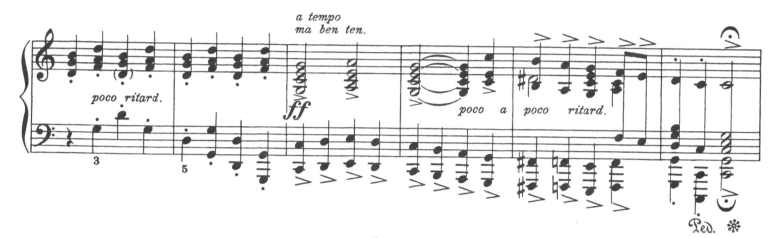

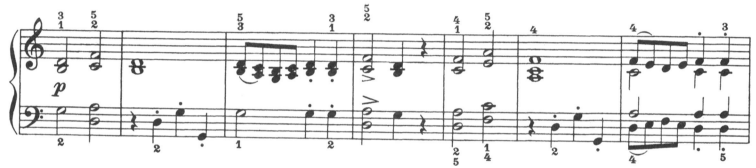

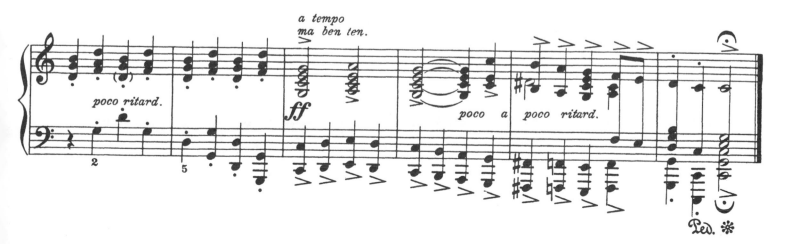

# March

from *Albumleaves for the Young*

Cornelius Gurlitt
Op. 101, No. 1

**Vivace ma non troppo**

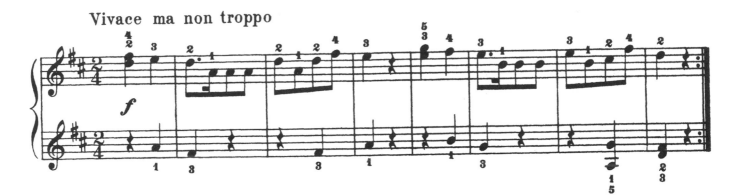

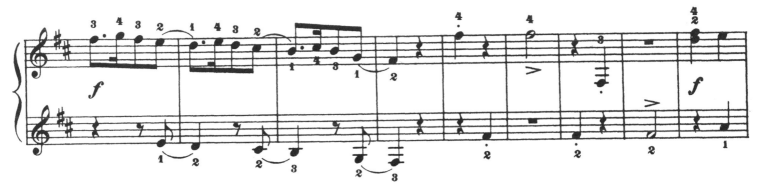

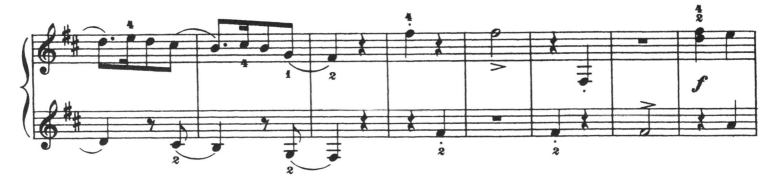

# Morning Prayer

from *Albumleaves for the Young*

Cornelius Gurlitt
Op. 101, No. 2

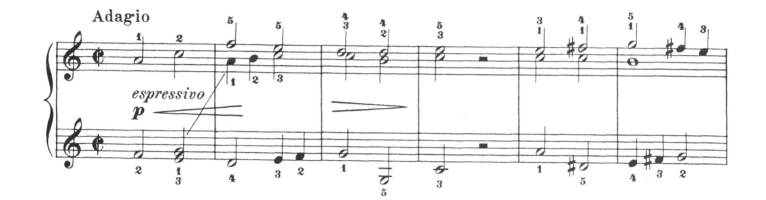

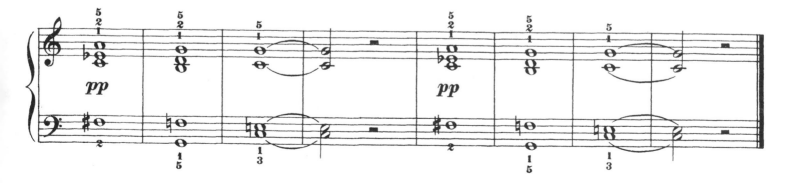

# By the Spring

from *Albumleaves for the Young*

Cornelius Gurlitt
Op. 101, No. 5

**Moderato, quasi Allegretto**

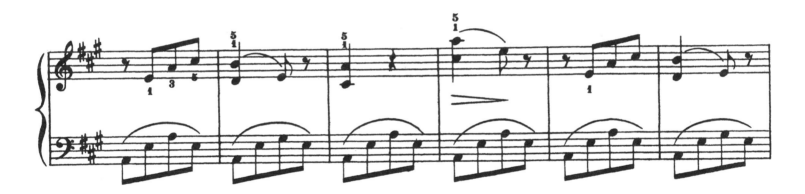

# The Fair

from *Albumleaves for the Young*

Cornelius Gurlitt
Op. 101, No. 8

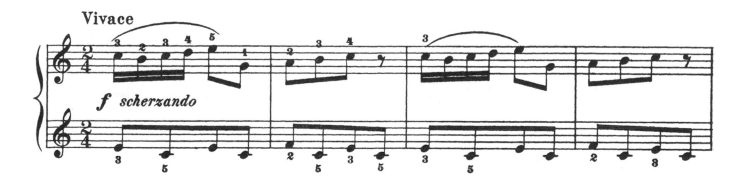

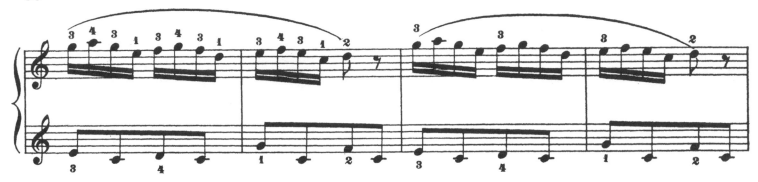

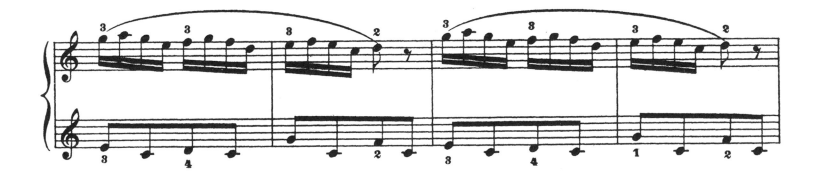

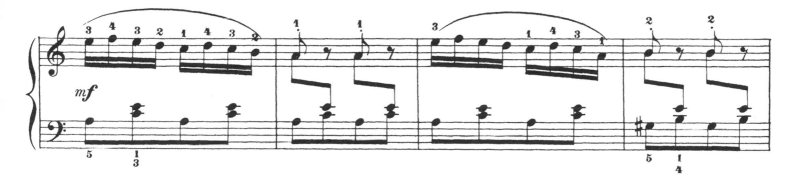

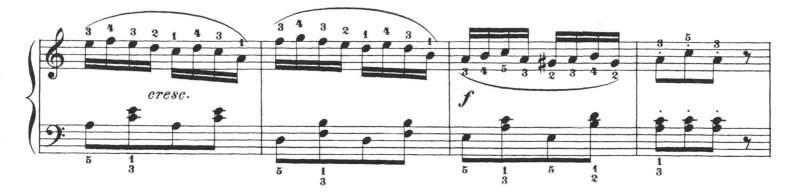

# Song without Words

from *Albumleaves for the Young*

Cornelius Gurlitt
Op. 101, No. 10

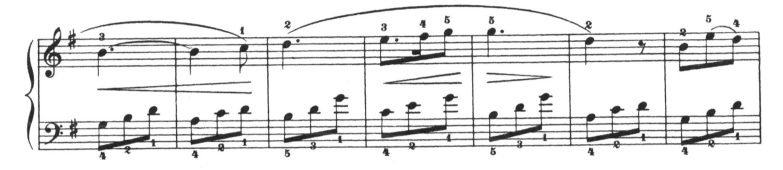

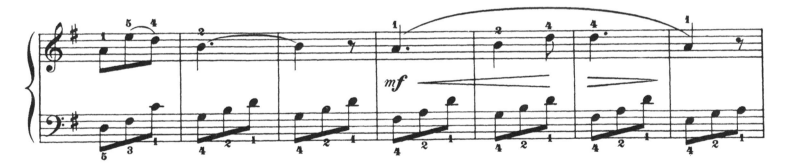

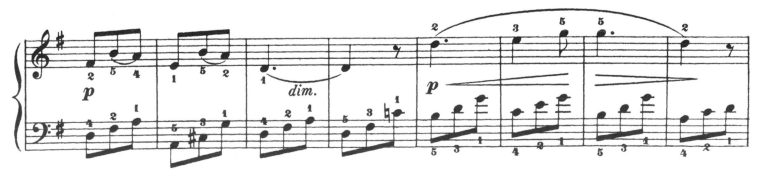

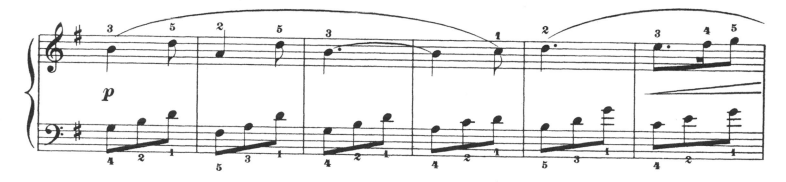

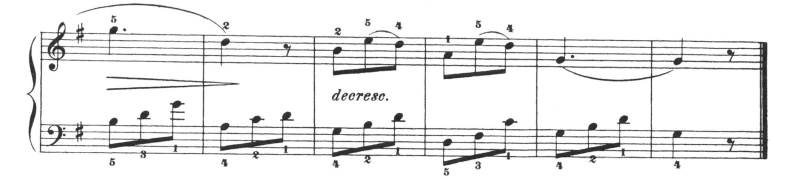

# Waltz
from *Albumleaves for the Young*

Cornelius Gurlitt
Op. 101, No. 11

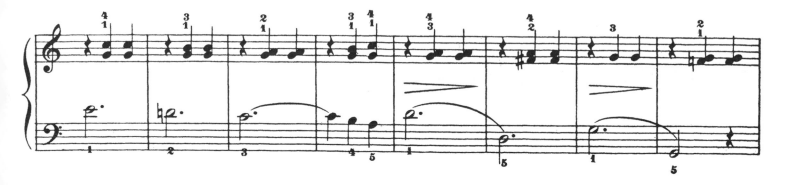

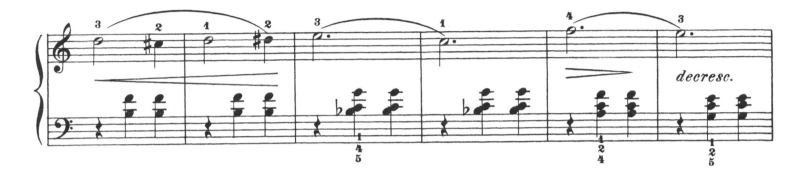

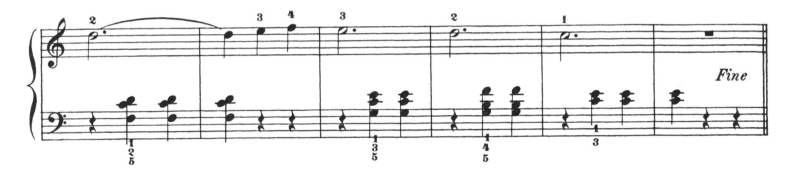

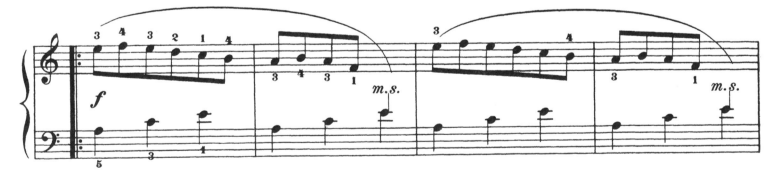

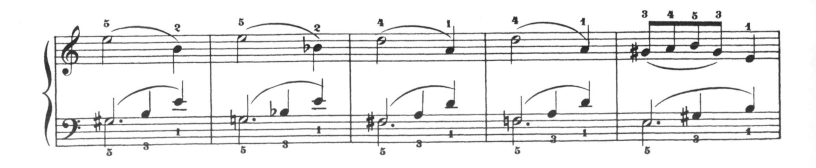

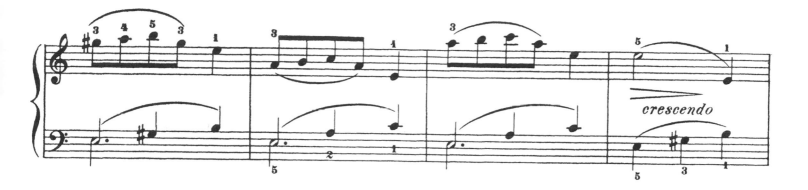

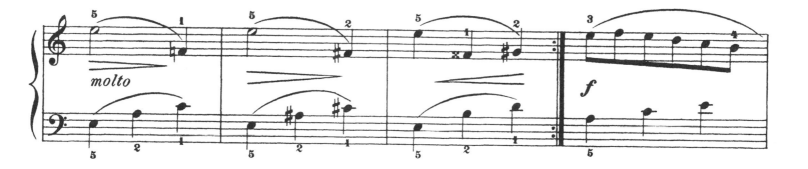

D.C. al Fine

# Grandfather's Birthday

from *Albumleaves for the Young*

Cornelius Gurlitt
Op. 101, No. 13

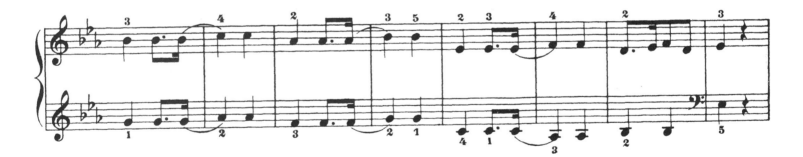

# Valse Noble

from *Albumleaves for the Young*

Cornelius Gurlitt
Op. 101, No. 14

**Moderato**

# Free Fancies

from *Albumleaves for the Young*

Cornelius Gurlitt
Op. 101, No. 17

# Sunday
from *Albumleaves for the Young*

Cornelius Gurlitt
Op. 101, No. 18

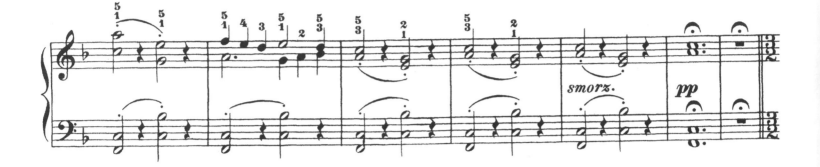

**Choral** { Praise the Lord, the Almighty King of Glory.
Lobe den Herren, den mächtigen König der Ehren.

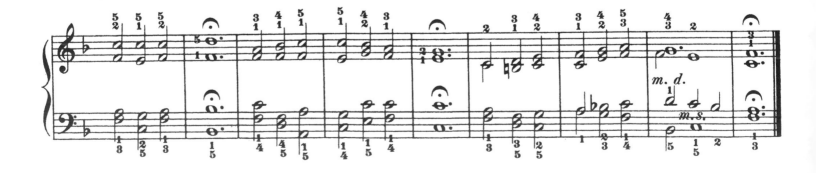

# Sarabande

from Suite in D minor

George Frideric Handel
HWV 437

## Variazione II

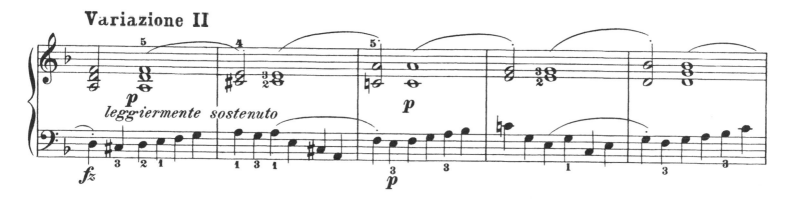

# Scampering
from *25 Studies*

Stephen Heller
Op. 47, No. 1

**Allegretto** ( ♩ = 80 )

# Lullaby

from *25 Studies*

Stephen Heller
Op. 47, No. 19

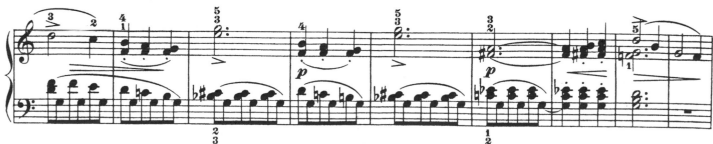

# 12 Easy Studies for the Piano

Louis Köhler
Op. 157

## 1.

## 2.

## 3.

## 4.

## 5.

# 6.

# 7.

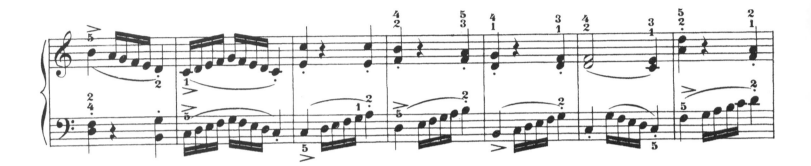

# 8.

## 9.

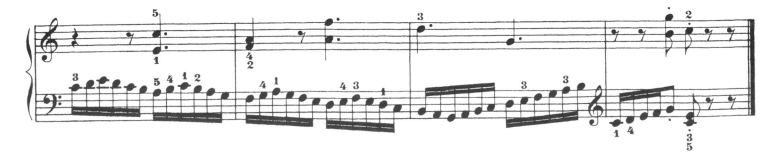

## 10.

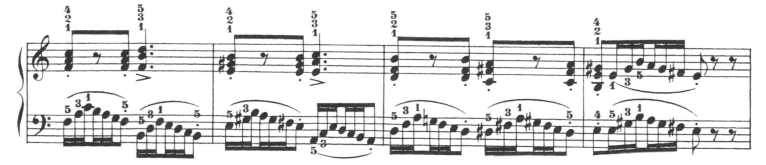

# 11.

## 12.

# The Clock
from *Scenes from Childhood*

Theodor Kullak
Op. 62, No. 2

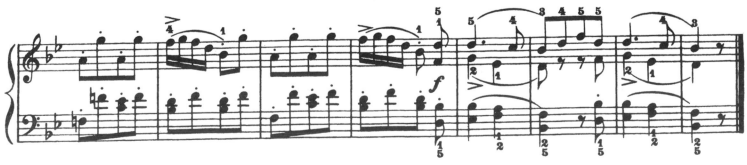

# The Alphabet

Felix Le Couppey
Op. 17

**Exercise**

**B.**

**Andantino** ($\textrm{♩}=66$)

**Study II**

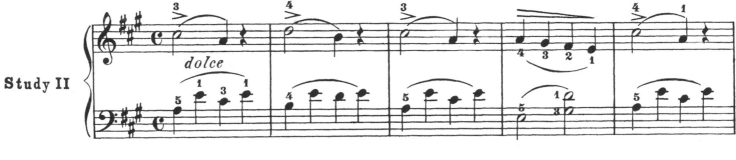

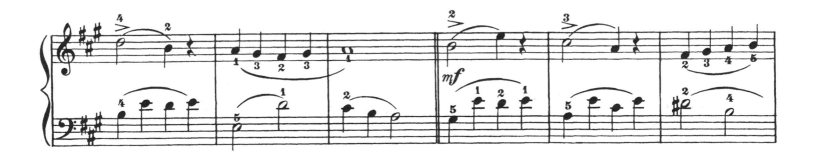

**Exercise**

C.

**Allegretto** ($\downarrow$ = 120)

Study III

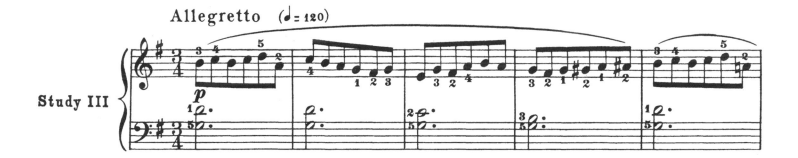

**Exercise**

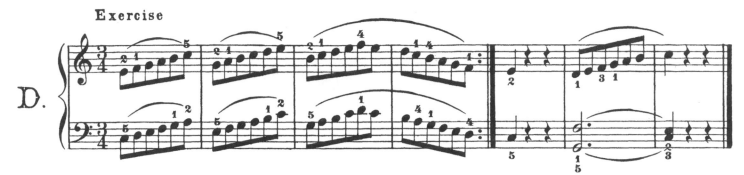

**Study IV**

Andantino ($\quad$ = 112)

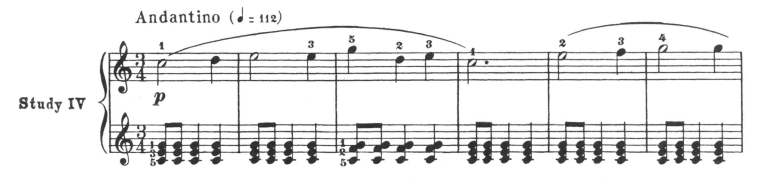

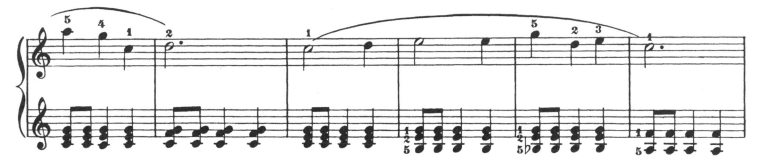

*D. C. al Fine*

Exercise

E.

Study V

Allegro (♩ = 126)

*f* Bourrée

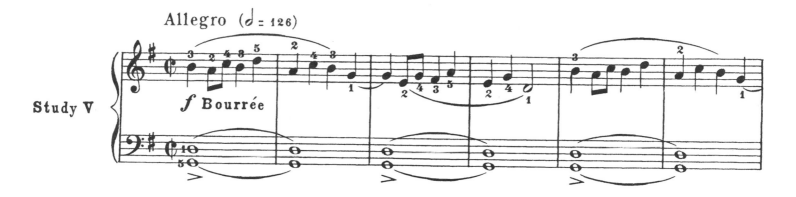

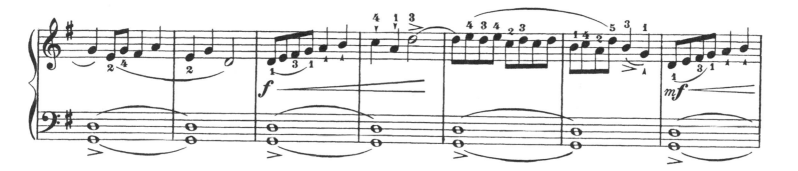

*pp*

*dimin.*

*ppp*

**Exercise**

F.

**Allegretto** (♩. = 76)

Study VI

Exercise

G.

Andantino (♩ = 100)

Study VII

*p legato*

*Fine*

*D.C. al Fine*

**Exercise**

**H.**

**Study VIII**

Moderato ($\quad$ = 104)

*dolce*

*Fine*

*mf*

*D.C. al Fine*

**Exercise**

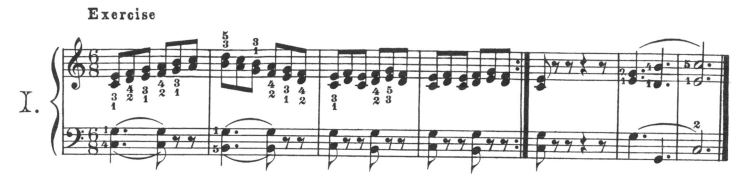

**Study IX**    Moderato (♩. = 76)

**Exercise**

**K.**

**Andantino** (♩ = 120)

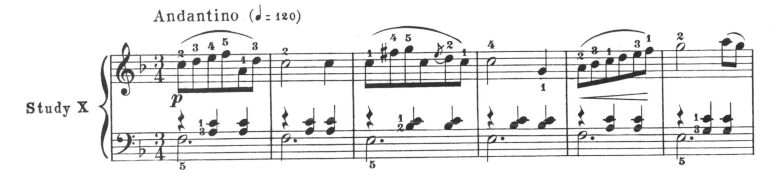

**Study X**

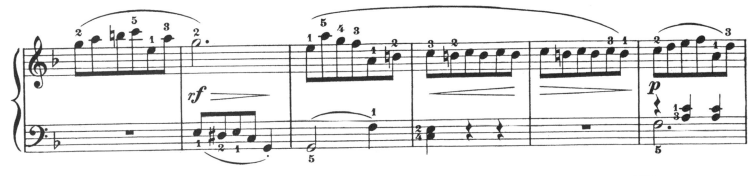

The composer did not write a piece for letter "J."

**Exercise**

**L.**

**Andante religioso** (♩= 66)

Study XI

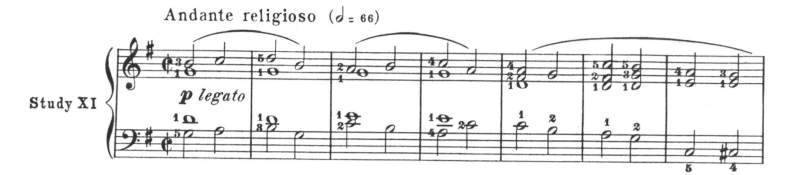

*p legato*

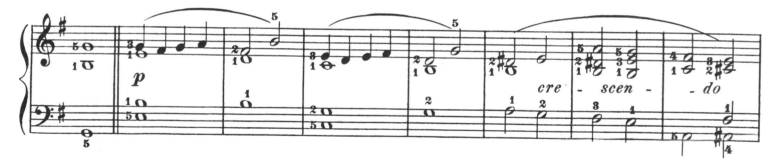

**Lento**

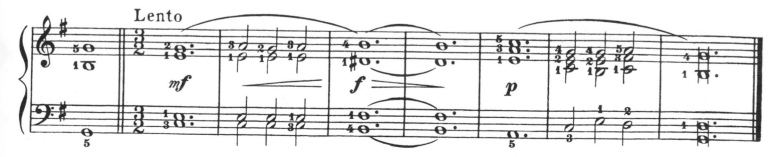

**Exercise**

**Study XII**

Allegretto (♩ = 152)

*Fine*

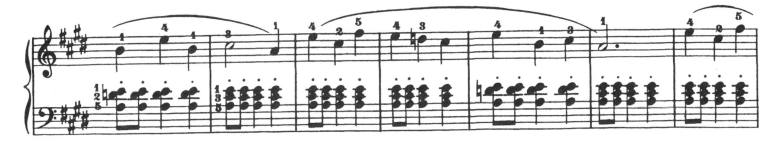

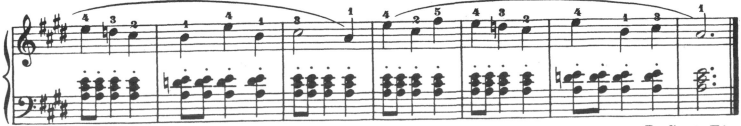

*D. C. al Fine*

Exercise

N.

Moderato (♩ = 126)

Study XIII

*p*

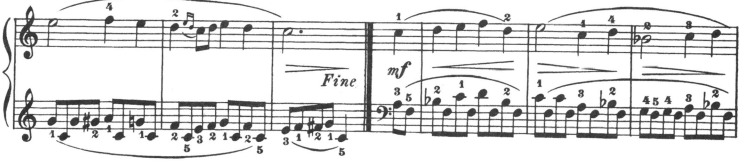

*Fine* *mf*

*p*

*cre - scen - do*

*D. C. al Fine*

**Exercise**

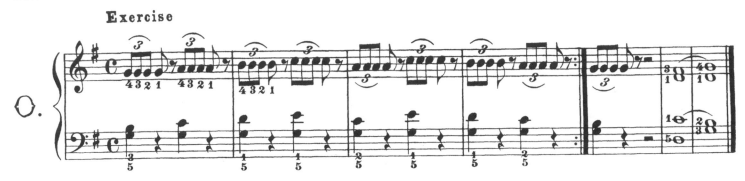

**Allegretto moderato** (♩ = 152)

Study XIV

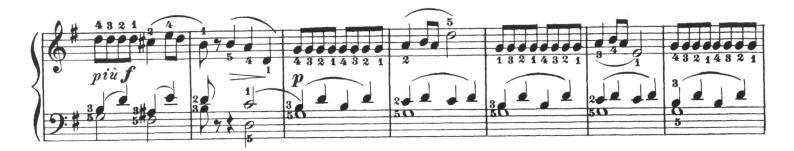

**Exercise**

**Study XV**

Moderato ($\quad= 88$)

**Exercise**

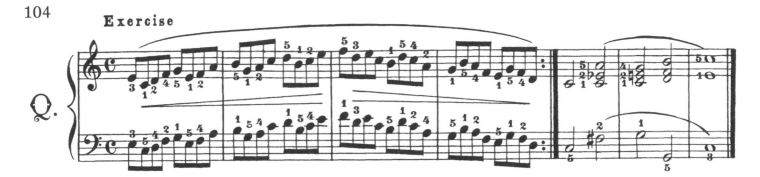

Q.

**Andante con moto** (♩ = 108)

Study XVI

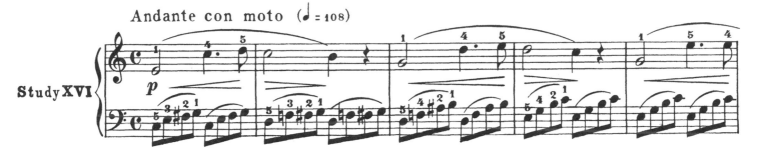

Exercise

Study XVII

Moderato (♩ = 152)

Chimes

**Exercise**

S.

**Study XVIII**

Moderato (♩ = 116)

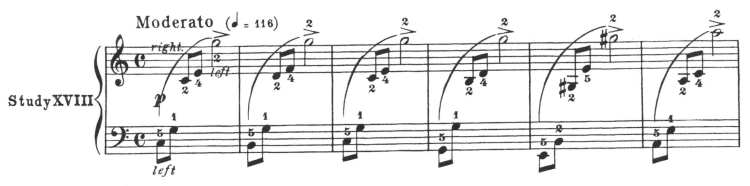

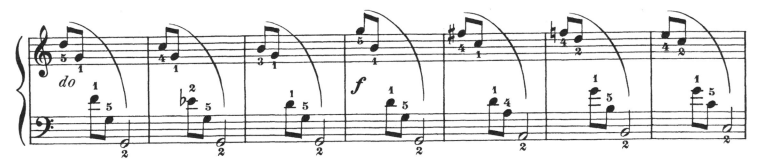

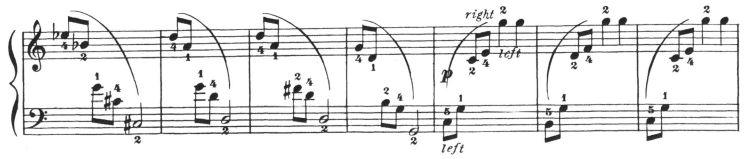

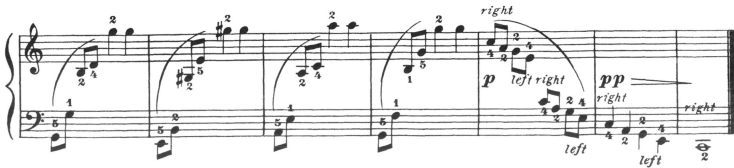

Exercise

T.

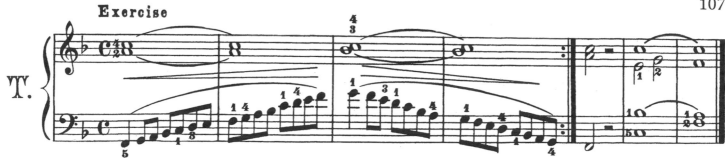

Moderato ( ♩ = 112 )

Study XIX

Exercise

Andantino ($\quad$ = 120)

Study XX

Exercise

Allegro (♩. = 80)

Study XXI

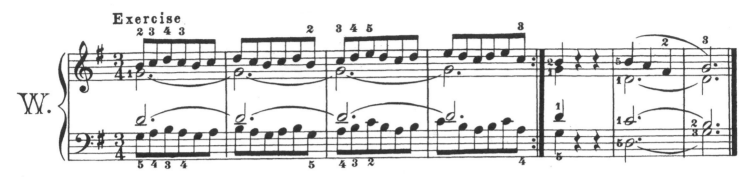

## Air on three notes by J. J. Rousseau

**Exercise**

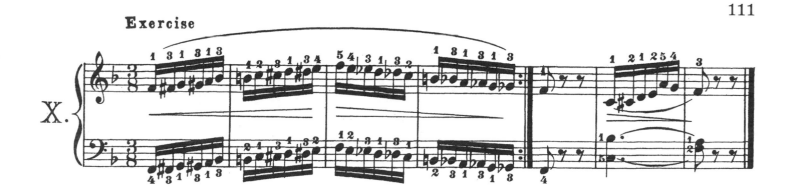

X.

**Allegretto** (♩.= 76)

Study XXIII

*p*

*Fine*

*cre - scen - do*

*D.C. al Fine*

**Exercise**

Y.

**Allegretto** ( ♩ = 76 )

Study **XXIV**

*p scherzando*

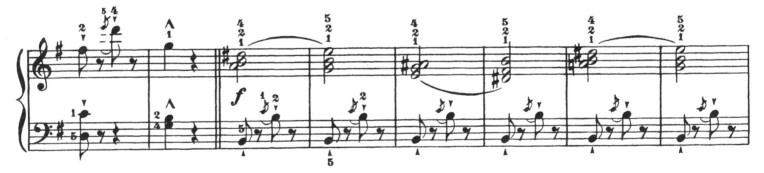

*p*

**Exercise**

**Z.**

**Allegro** (♩. = 76)

**Study XXV**

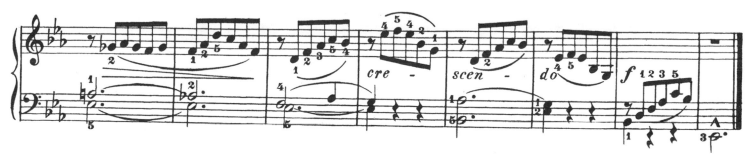

# Minuet
## in G Major

Christian Petzold
BWV Appendix 114

# Minuet
## in G minor

Christian Petzold
BWV Appendix 115

# Sonatina
## in C Major

Carl Reinecke
Op. 136, No. 1

**Primo Tempo**

**Scherzino**
Vivace

**Alla Polacca**

# Sonatina
## in G Major

Carl Reinecke
Op. 136, No. 2

**Allegro moderato**

## Menuetto

## Rondino

Vivace

# March

from *Miniatures*

Hugo Reinhold
Op. 39, No. 1

**Nicht zu schnell und sehr rhythmisch**
Allegro non troppo e ben ritmato

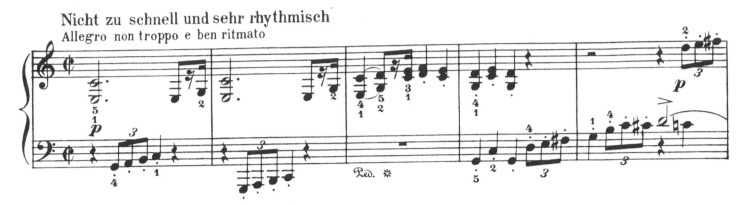

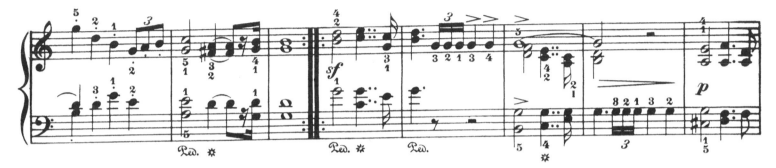

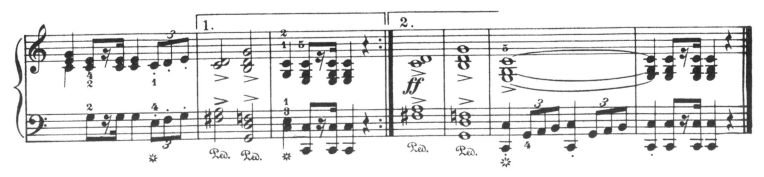

# Hungarian Dance
from *Miniatures*

Hugo Reinhold
Op. 39, No. 9

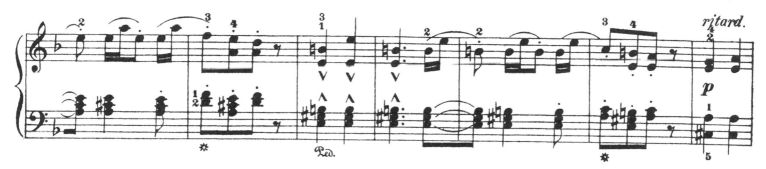

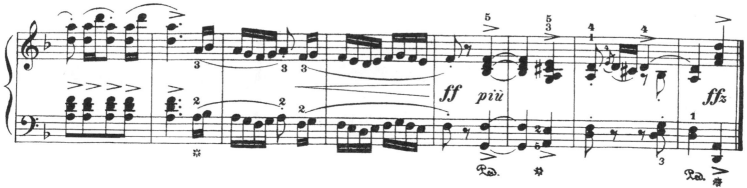

# Gypsy Song

from *Miniatures*

Hugo Reinhold
Op. 39, No. 13

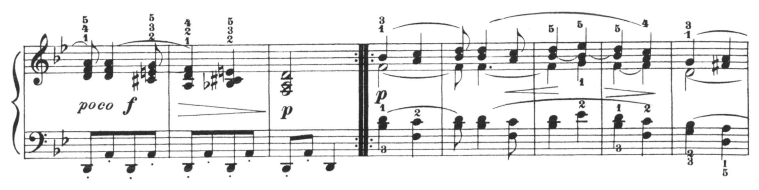

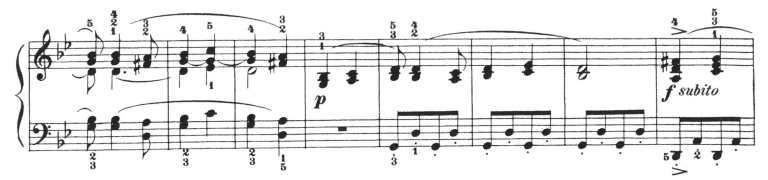

# Melodie
### (Melody)
#### from *Album for the Young*

Robert Schumann
Op. 68, No. 1

# Soldatenmarsch

(Soldiers' March)

from *Album for the Young*

Robert Schumann
Op. 68, No. 2

# Trällerliedchen

(Humming Song)

from *Album for the Young*

Robert Schumann
Op. 68, No. 3

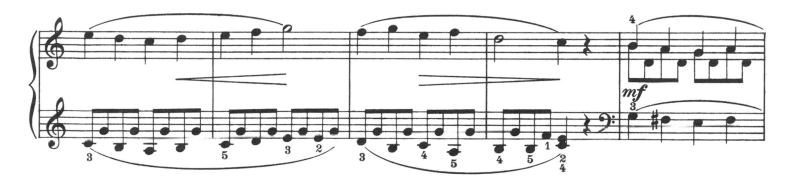

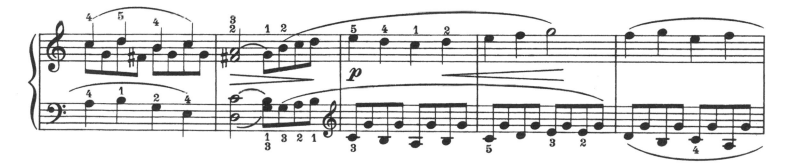

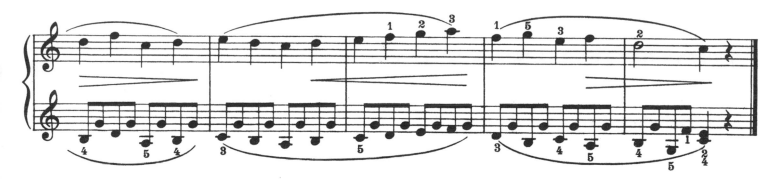

# Chorale
## (Choral)
### from *Album for the Young*

Robert Schumann
Op. 68, No. 4

# Stückchen
(Little Piece)
from *Album for the Young*

Robert Schumann
Op. 68, No. 5

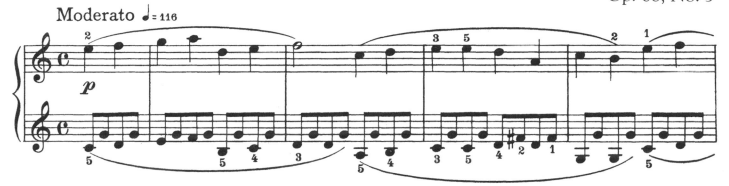

# Jägerliedchen

### (Hunting Song)
from *Album for the Young*

Robert Schumann
Op. 68, No. 7

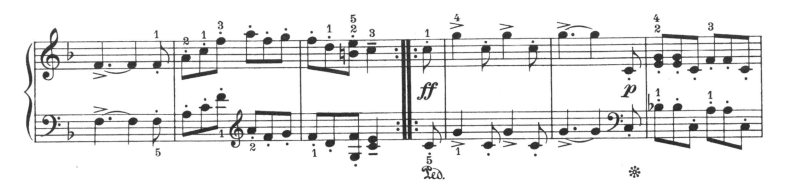

# Wilder Reiter
(The Wild Horseman)
from *Album for the Young*

Robert Schumann
Op. 68, No. 8

# Fröhlicher Landmann von der Arbeit zurükkehrend

(The Happy Farmer Returning from Work)

from *Album for the Young*

Robert Schumann
Op. 68, No. 10

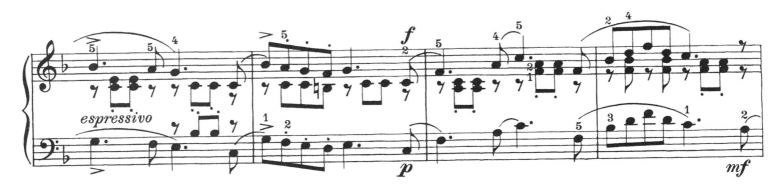

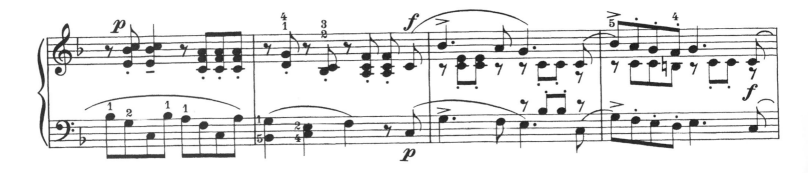

# Sicilianisch

(Sicilienne)

from *Album for the Young*

Robert Schumann
Op. 68, No. 11

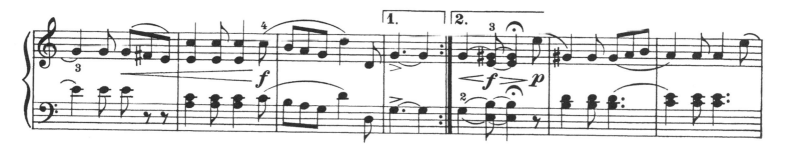

*D.C. senza repetizione al Fine*

# Kliene Studie
(Little Study)

from *Album for the Young*

Robert Schumann
Op. 68, No. 14

★Originally in 6/8 time. The editor has altered the notation to $\mathbf{C}$ (i.e. two measures in one) in order to indicate with greater clarity the rhythmical pulse of the piece.

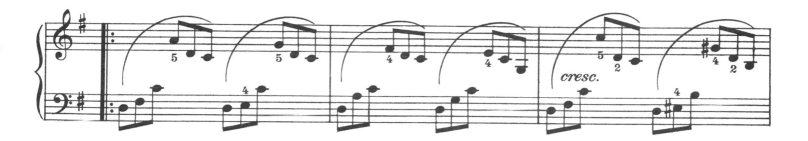

# Erster Verlust
(First Loss)
from *Album for the Young*

Robert Schumann
Op. 68, No. 16

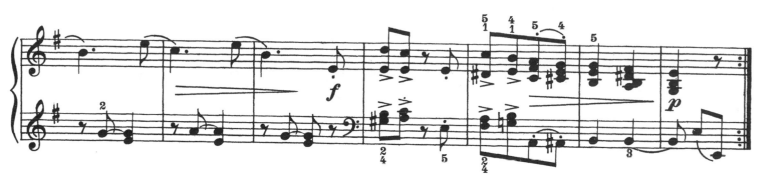

# Schnitterliedchen
### (The Reaper's Song)
#### from *Album for the Young*

Robert Schumann
Op. 68, No. 18

# 12 Very Easy and Melodious Studies

## A Pleasant Morning

Louis Streabbog
Op. 63

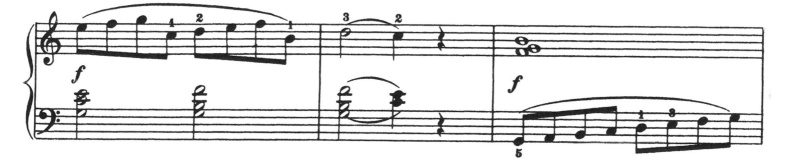

# Soldiers' March

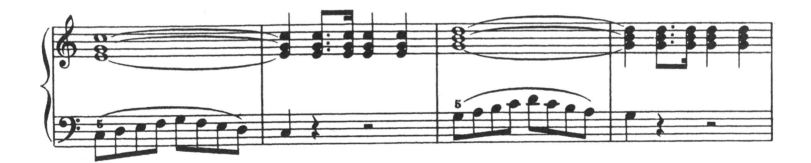

# On the Green

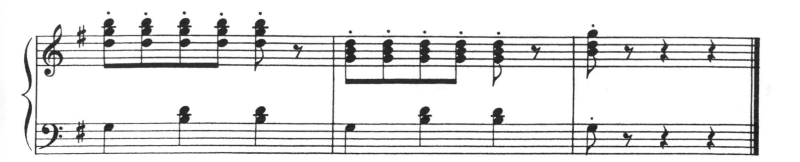

# In the Swing

**Andante**

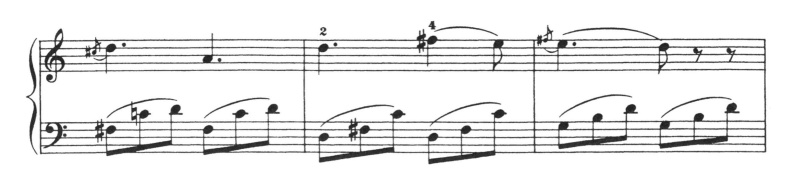

# In a Hurry

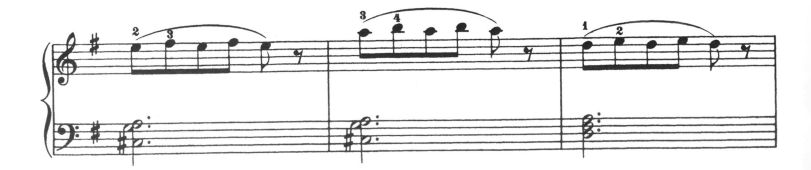

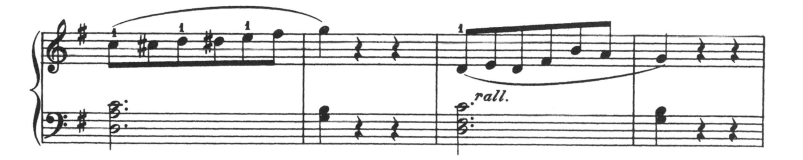

# Distant Bells

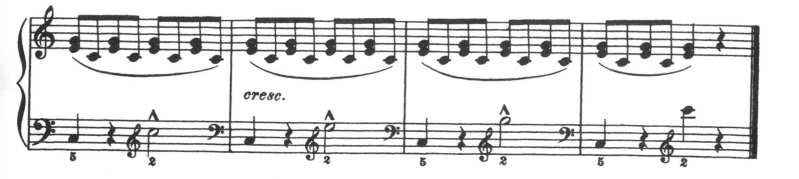

# By the Seaside

# Hop Scotch Polka

8.

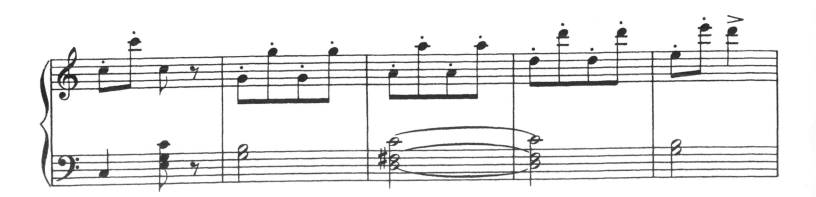

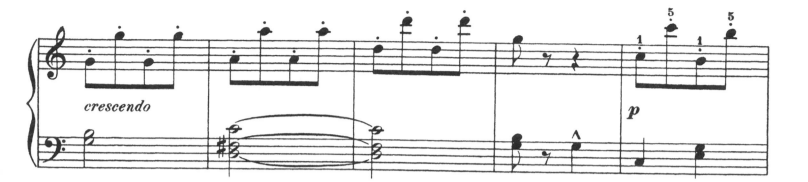

# The Stubborn Rocking Horse

9.

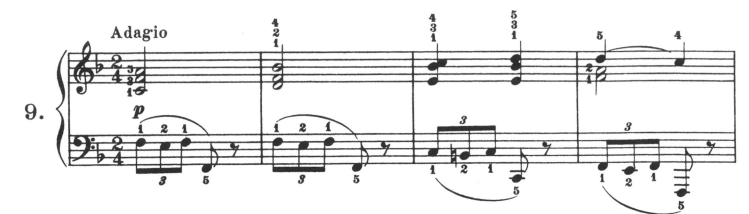

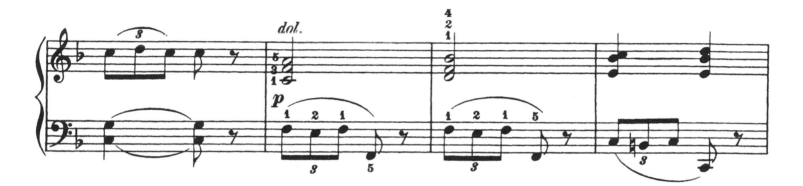

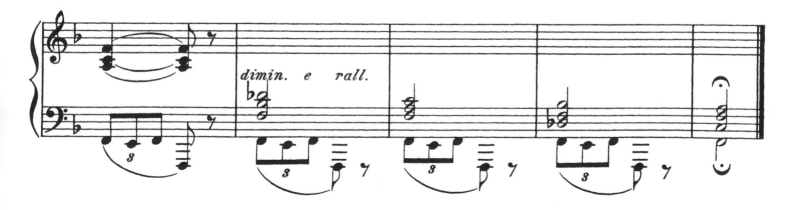

# A Sad Story

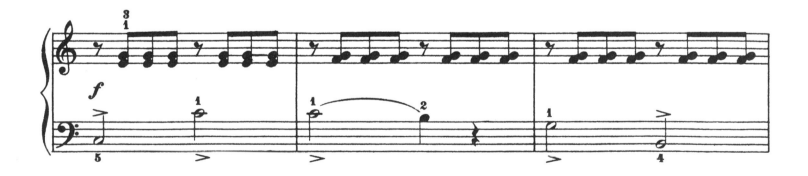

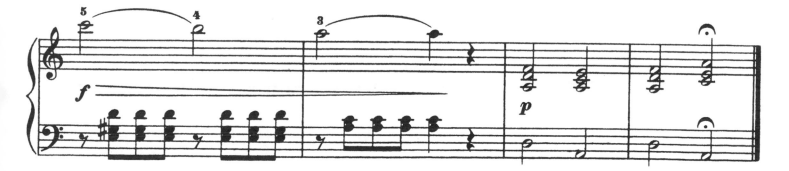

# Chasing Butterflies

11.

# Vacation Time

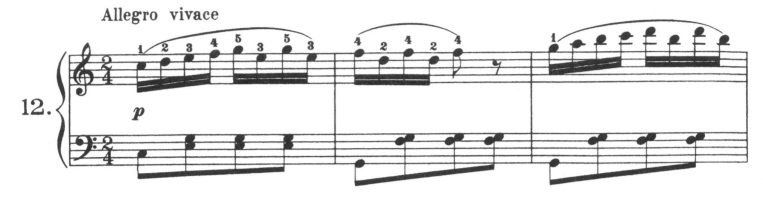

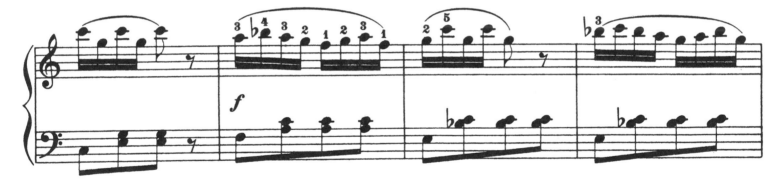

# 12 Easy and Melodious Studies

## Leap-Frog

Louis Streabbog
Op. 64

# Bees in the Clover

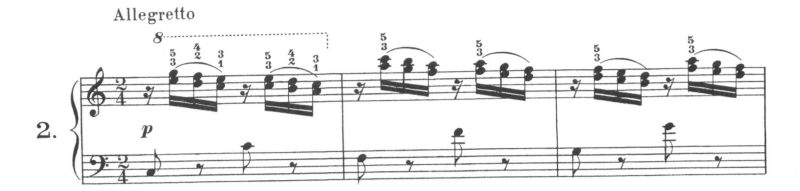

2.

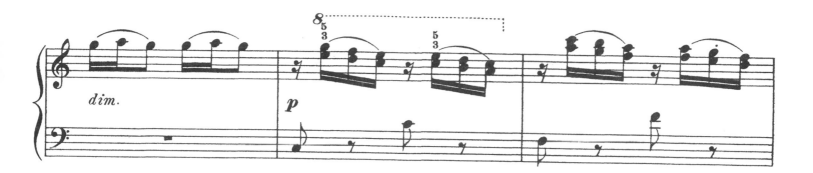

# Jack Frost

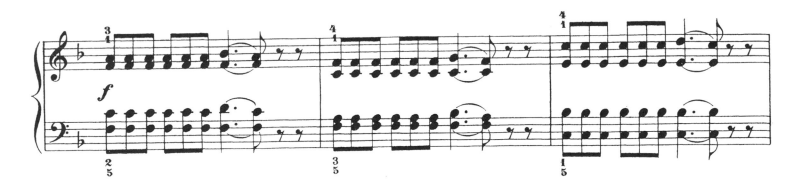

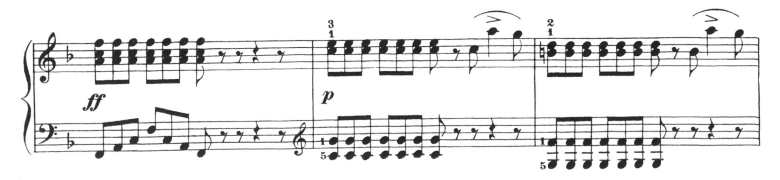

# The Orphan

# Rope-Skipping

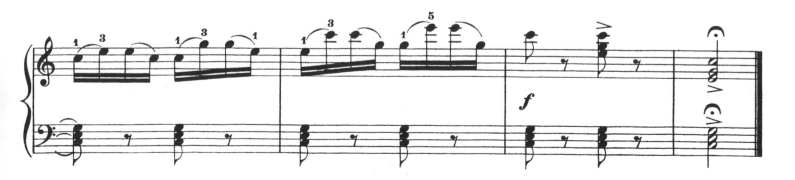

# Swaying Boughs

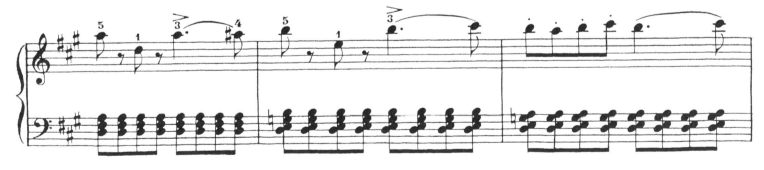

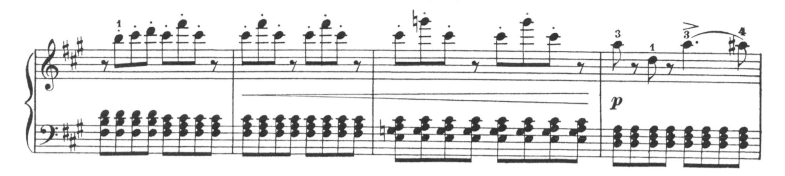

# Wild Flowers

# The Woodpecker

# The Whirlwind

Allegro moderato

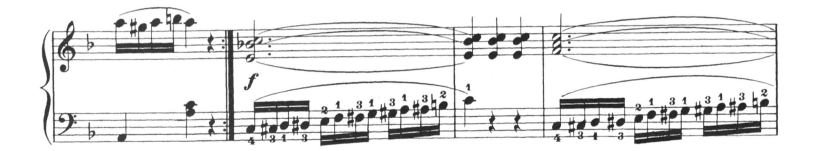

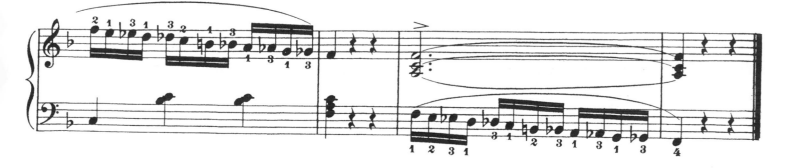

# The Rope-Dancer

# The Cadets

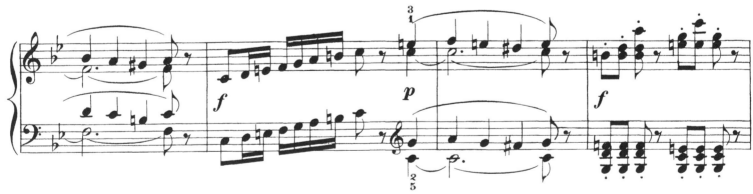

# Up and Down

# Morning Prayer

from *Album for the Young*

Pyotr Il'yich Tchaikovsky
Op. 39, No. 1

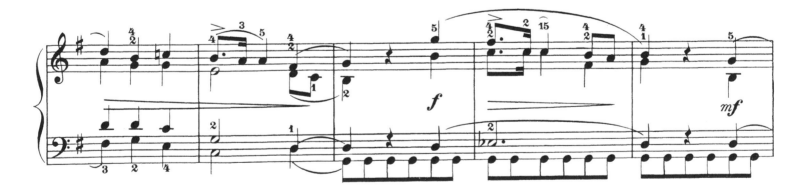

# The Sick Doll

from *Album for the Young*

Pyotr Il'yich Tchaikovsky
Op. 39, No. 6

*marcato il basso*

# The Doll's Burial

from *Album for the Young*

Pyotr Il'yich Tchaikovsky
Op. 39, No. 7

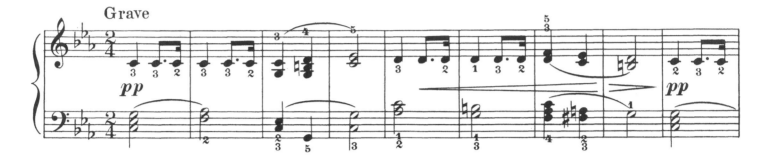

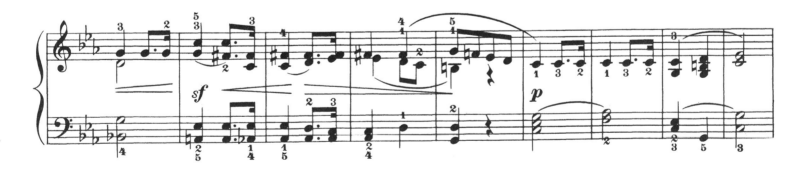

# In Church

from *Album for the Young*

Pyotr Il'yich Tchaikovsky
Op. 39, No. 24

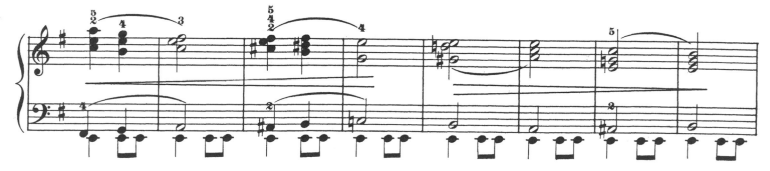